State of CONFUSION

Buffy Silverman

Raintree

Schools Library and Infomation Services

www.raintreepublishers.co.uk

Visit our website to find out more information about **Raintree** books.

To order:

☎ Phone 44 (0) 1865 888112

📄 Send a fax to 44 (0) 1865 314091

💻 Visit the Raintree Bookshop at **www.raintreepublishers.co.uk** to browse our catalogue and order online.

First published in Great Britain by Raintree,
Halley Court, Jordan Hill, Oxford OX2 8EJ,
part of Harcourt Education.
Raintree is a registered trademark of Harcourt
Education Ltd.

Editorial: Nancy Dickmann and Catherine Veitch
Design: Philippa Jenkins and Q2A Creative
Picture Research: Ruth Blair
Production: Alison Parsons

Originated by Modern Age
Printed and bound in China by Leo Paper Group

ISBN 978-1-4062-0741-5 (hardback)
12 11 10 09 08
10 9 8 7 6 5 4 3 2 1

ISBN 978-1-4062-0755-2 (paperback)
12 11 10 09 08
10 9 8 7 6 5 4 3 2 1

**British Library Cataloguing in Publication
Data**
Silverman, Buffy
State of confusion. - (Fusion)
1. Solids - Juvenile literature
2. Liquids - Juvenile literature
3. Gases - Juvenile literature
I. Title 530.4
A full catalogue record for this book is available from
the British Library.

Acknowledgements
The author and publisher are grateful to the
following for permission to reproduce copyright
material: Corbis pp. **18** (Royalty Free), **20-21**
(Roulier/Turiot/photocuisine), **27** (José F. Poblete);
FLPA p.**17** (Rinie Van Muers/Foto Natura); Harcourt
Education/Tudor Photography pp.**24**, **25**; NHPA
p.**22** (ANT Photo Library); photolibrary.com pp.**5**
(Imagestate Ltd), **6**, **11** (Phototake Inc), **12-13**
(Pacific Stock), **23** (Pacific Stock); Science Photo
Library pp.**8** (John Mead), **14** (Martyn F. Chillmaid),
28-29 (Paul Silverman/Fundamental Photos).

Cover photograph of oil and water mixing
reproduced with permission of photolibrary.com.

Illustrations by Peter Geissler and Mark Preston.

Every effort has been made to contact copyright
holders of any material reproduced in this book. Any
omissions will be rectified in subsequent printings if
notice is given to the publishers.

The publishers would like to thank Nancy Harris and
Harold Pratt for their assistance with the preparation
of this book.

Contents

Some words are printed in bold, **like this.** You can find out what they mean on page 30. You can also look in the box at the bottom of the page where they first appear.

What's the matter?

You ride along a trail. The wind blows in your face. You hop over a rock and soar through the air. You speed down a hill. At the bottom you splash through a puddle. Water and mud coat your bike.

Everything you see on the trail is made of **matter**. Your bike is made of matter. The rocks and leaves are made of matter. Puddles and mud are made of matter. The air that blows is made of matter.

What is matter? Matter takes up space. Matter can be weighed. A speck of dust and a giant boulder are made of matter. Air and water are made of matter. Your clothes and your bike are made of matter. Even you are made of matter! Everything on Earth is made of matter.

Mud covers your bike. The mud, your bike, and you are made of matter.

Building matter

You paddle a boat in quiet waters. Suddenly the river
narrows. Water churns and bubbles. You slide over rocks.
You streak past tree branches.

*Everything in a river is
made of matter. Matter
is made of tiny particles
that you cannot see.*

Everything in the river is made of **matter**. Matter is made of tiny **particles** (parts) that you cannot see. The smallest particles are called **atoms**. The water, rocks, trees, and fish are made of atoms. All matter is made of atoms.

Atoms are the building blocks of matter. Atoms join together to make matter. There are more than 100 different types of atom. An atom can combine with another atom of the same type. An atom also can join with different types of atom. Atoms combine in thousands of different ways. They combine and make matter.

Small fact!

Hydrogen is the smallest atom. About five trillion hydrogen atoms can fit on the head of a pin!

Water is made of two types of atom. Water is made of hydrogen and oxygen atoms.

0   0

H

key

H = hydrogen
O = oxygen

States of matter

All **matter** is made of **atoms**. But there are different **states** (forms) of matter. Matter can be a **solid**. Matter can be a **liquid**. Matter can be a **gas**. Matter can change from one state to another.

If you touch a rock, it feels hard. Rocks are solids. A solid is matter that keeps its shape. The **particles** (tiny parts) in a solid are packed tightly together.

Strong solid

Diamonds are the hardest solids. Diamonds can cut glass and steel.

8

Rocks are solid. They keep their shape. ↑

gas matter that spreads apart and fills any container
liquid matter that flows and can change shape
solid substance with a definite shape
state form of matter

Characteristics of solids

	Solid	
Shape		A solid has its own shape.
Change of shape		It is hard to change a solid's shape.
Size		A solid is a specific size.

Imagine people crammed in a lift. They cannot move around. The particles of a solid crowd together like people in a lift. They pull towards each other and hold together.

Solids usually feel hard. Solids hold their shape unless something is done to change them. Pressing on clay changes its shape. It flattens. The shape of a solid only changes if something pushes or pulls it. Even if its shape changes, a solid always takes up the same amount of space.

Liquids

Have you ever spilled juice? It flows across the table. It drips on to the floor.

Juice is a **liquid**. It does not have its own shape. It is not round like a ball. It is not tall like a pole.

If you pour juice into a glass, the juice takes the shape of the glass. Liquid in a tall, thin glass has a tall, thin shape. Liquid in a wide glass has a wide shape. Liquids take the shape of their container.

Characteristics of solids and liquids

	Solid		Liquid	
Shape		A solid has its own shape.		A liquid does not have its own shape.
Change of shape		It is hard to change a solid's shape.		A liquid changes shape when poured into a new container.
Size		A solid is a specific size.		A liquid has a specific **volume**.

The **particles** (tiny parts) in liquids do not pull together as tightly as a **solid**. Imagine the doors of an elevator opening. People flow out into the hallway. Particles in a liquid act the same way. They always move around. They slide under, over, and around each other. That is why liquids flow.

Pour some liquid into a container. The container might be tall or short. But there is still the same amount of liquid. Even if the shape changes, liquids always take up the same amount of space.

Liquids take the shape of their container.

Gases

A hot-air balloon rises in the sky. What fills the balloon?
Air! The balloon looks empty. But it is filled with heated air.

Air is **matter**. It is made of **gases**. You cannot see some
gases. But you can see that gases push out the sides of a
balloon. When there is no gas in it, a balloon lies flat.

Gases are all around us. We breathe gases in and out
of our bodies. A gas can take any shape. It spreads out
in whatever space it is in. It fills any size container.
If a container is opened, gases escape.

Characteristics of solids, liquids, and gases

	Solid	Liquid	Gas
Shape	A solid has its own shape.	A liquid does not have its own shape.	A gas does not have its own shape.
Change of shape	It is hard to change a solid's shape.	A liquid changes shape when poured into a new container.	A gas takes the shape of its container.
Size	A solid is a specific size.	A liquid has a specific **volume**.	A gas spreads out to fill its container.

press pres

The tiny **particles** in gases spread far apart. The particles are always moving. Imagine a crowd leaving a building. People move quickly down the street. They travel in every direction. The particles in a gas spread apart like this. They move quickly. They go in any direction.

Gas can be **compressed** (squashed). A gas is pushed into a smaller container. The particles are pushed closer together. They are compressed.

Gas fills a hot-air balloon and makes it rise.

Changing states

Sugar is a **solid**. It holds its shape. But sugar can change **states**. If sugar is heated, it changes state. It turns from solid to **liquid**. This is called **melting**.

What happens when liquid sugar cools? It hardens. It changes from a liquid to a solid. People make sweets by melting sugar and letting it harden.

Turn up the temperature

Solids melt at different temperatures. Ice melts at 0 °C (32 °F). Sugar melts at 179 °C (454 °F). To melt a diamond, it must be heated to 3,550 °C (6,422 °F)!

energy ability to make something happen
melt reach a temperature at which a solid changes to a liquid

Usually **matter** stays in the same state. A solid stays a solid. A liquid stays a liquid. A **gas** remains a gas. But when matter is heated or cooled, it can change. A solid can turn to liquid. A liquid can become a gas.

When matter changes state, it is still made of the same **particles**. When a solid is heated, its particles get more **energy**. Energy makes things happen. It can make objects move. The particles move faster. They slide past one another and spread apart. The solid turns into a liquid.

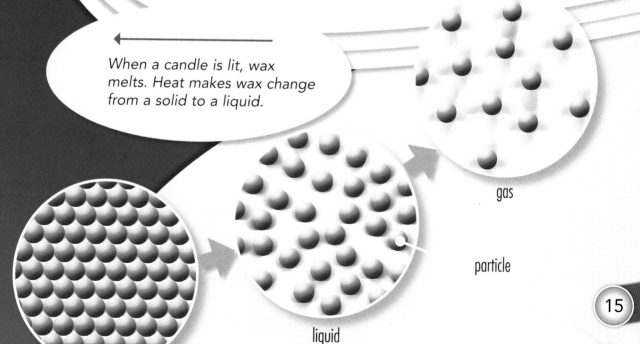

When a candle is lit, wax melts. Heat makes wax change from a solid to a liquid.

gas

particle

liquid

solid

When a solid object is heated, it turns from solid to liquid to gas.

15

Ice, water, and vapour

A polar bear runs across ice. In the summer the bear swims across. The **solid** ice can change into **liquid** water.

When water **freezes** it turns from a liquid to a solid. Water freezes when it is cold. If the temperature is 0 °C (32 °F) or below, liquid water turns to solid ice. Above 0 °C (32 °F) the ice warms and **melts**. It changes back to liquid water.

Find a puddle on a hot day. If the Sun is out, the puddle disappears. Where does the water go? The heat of the Sun makes water **evaporate**. Liquid water changes into a **gas**. The gas is called water **vapour**. The vapour goes into the air. You cannot see it, but the water is still there.

Water changes from liquid to gas when it is heated. As the gas cools it changes back to liquid.

Boil over

Water **boils** at 100 °C (212 °F). It turns to vapour (gas) when it boils.

Polar bears walk across ice in winter. In summer the ice melts and the bears swim.

boil reach a temperature at which a liquid changes to a gas
evaporate change from liquid into a gas
freeze change from liquid to solid by loss of heat

Out of thin air

The air you breathe has water vapour. Pour cold water in a glass and wait. Soon, the outside of the glass gets wet. Where did this water come from? The air! Water vapour in air turns to liquid when it is cooled. The cold glass makes water vapour near by turn to liquid water. The water vapour **condenses**. It changes from a gas to a liquid.

condense cause a gas to change to a liquid

Moving particles

When **matter** changes its form, the **particles** move apart or come together. Ice is hard because its particles are packed close together.

When ice is heated, water particles get **energy**. The particles move faster. When they move they do not stick together as much. They start to flow apart. The **solid** ice changes. It turns into **liquid** water.

More heat is needed to make liquid water turn into water **vapour**. Heat gives particles energy. That makes particles move faster. Particles in a **gas** can move in any direction.

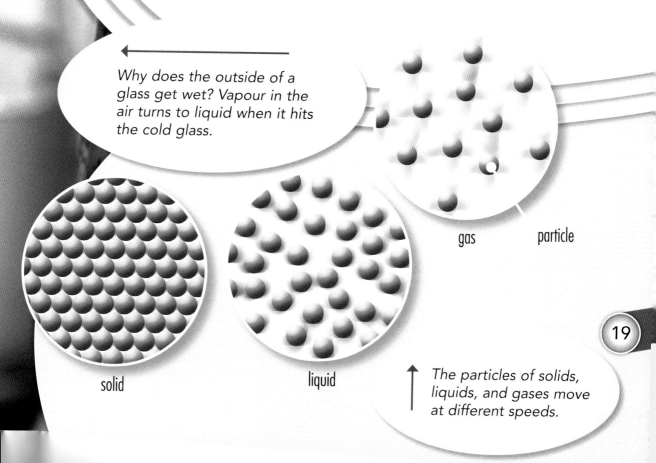

Why does the outside of a glass get wet? Vapour in the air turns to liquid when it hits the cold glass.

gas

particle

solid

liquid

The particles of solids, liquids, and gases move at different speeds.

19

Mixed-up matter

A bowl of vegetable soup sits on a table. The soup takes the shape of the bowl. You can pour it from one container to another. Is it a **liquid**? You put your hand over the soup. **Vapour** rises. The vapour makes your hand wet. Is it a **gas**? You slip your spoon into the bowl. You stir the vegetables. They hold their shape. Is this soup a **solid**?

Vegetable soup is a **mixture**. It contains liquids and solids. Water vapour rising from soup is a gas. Many materials have mixtures of different **states** (forms) of **matter**.

Seawater is another mixture. It is a mixture of salt and water. Solid salt is dissolved in liquid water. If seawater **evaporates** (changes from liquid to gas), salt is left behind.

Slurp up some soup! Are you eating solids, liquids, or gases?

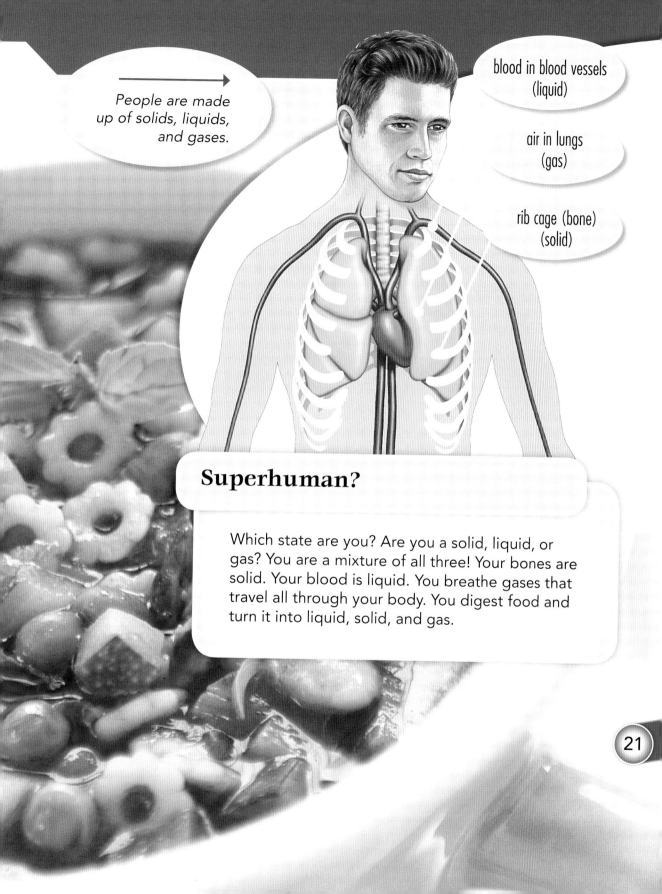

People are made up of solids, liquids, and gases.

blood in blood vessels (liquid)

air in lungs (gas)

rib cage (bone) (solid)

Superhuman?

Which state are you? Are you a solid, liquid, or gas? You are a mixture of all three! Your bones are solid. Your blood is liquid. You breathe gases that travel all through your body. You digest food and turn it into liquid, solid, and gas.

Matter mysteries

You climb a sand dune at the beach. Wind blows. Sand slides down. It looks like a river flowing. You put sand in a bucket. It takes the shape of the container. You can pour sand. Is sand a **liquid**?

Some **matter** is hard to classify. Take a closer look at sand. Each grain feels hard. A grain of sand does not change shape. If you could split it in half, the pieces would hold their shape. Each grain of sand is a **solid**. Although a bucketful of sand acts like a liquid, it is not a liquid. The bucket contains many tiny solids.

Powerful strike

Lightning can turn sand to liquid. The lightning heats sand and **melts** it.

Wind blows sand. The sand looks like waves. Sand is not a liquid. Sand is a solid.

lava liquid rock flowing out of a volcano

↑ *Heat turns solid rock into liquid. The liquid flows out of a volcano. It is red-hot lava.*

Rocks are solids. But rocks can turn into liquid! Inside Earth, rock is heated to very high temperatures. Heat turns rock to a liquid. The liquid is called **magma**. When a volcano erupts, liquid rock flows out. Above ground it is called **lava**.

More mysterious matter

Have you ever mixed cornflour and water? The material you make is sometimes called oobleck.

When you stir oobleck, it feels stiff. It sticks together in blocks. Break off a clump of oobleck. It breaks into pieces like a **solid**. Squeeze it. The clump feels hard. It holds its shape. Is oobleck a solid?

Make your own oobleck

Put 200 ml (1 cup) of cornflour in a bowl. Add two drops of food colouring. Slowly add 200 ml (1 cup) of water and stir. If it is too stiff, add more water. How is your oobleck like a solid? How is it like a liquid?

When you punch oobleck, it feels like a solid.

Oobleck drips
from your hand
like a liquid.

After a short time, the oobleck starts to spread. It flows like a **liquid** and spreads out. Try lifting the oobleck. It flows through your fingers. It drips like a liquid.

Oobleck is a special kind of liquid. Put some in your hand. It flows and spreads apart. But when you press on oobleck, it acts like a solid. It forms hard clumps. It holds its shape.

Liquid or solid?

All **liquids** can flow and change shape. Water flows quickly. Thick liquids, such as honey, flow slowly. **Tar** is a liquid. Tar is much thicker than honey. It flows 100 billion times more slowly than water!

Tar is made from coal or oil. It is used to pave roads. It looks and feels like a **solid**. Tar appears to keep its shape. It can be broken with a hammer.

Thomas Parnell was a scientist. He lived in Australia. He wanted to learn if tar was a liquid or solid. In 1927 he started an experiment. He heated tar and poured it into a funnel. The funnel was sealed shut. He let the tar settle for three years. Then, he broke open the stem of the funnel. He left the tar to drip out.

It took 8 years for the first drop to fall. In 70 years, only 8 drops have fallen. The tar drop experiment is still going on.

Is tar a liquid? It has slowly changed shape. It flows. It is a very thick liquid!

People pave roads with tar. Tar flows slowly because it is a very thick liquid.

Sort the states

Consider each material on this page. Is it a **solid**, **liquid**, or **gas**? Is it a **mixture**?

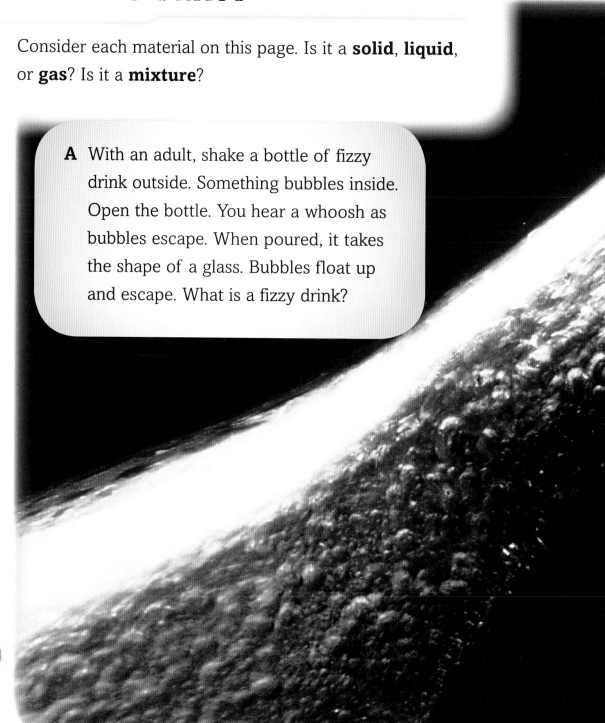

A With an adult, shake a bottle of fizzy drink outside. Something bubbles inside. Open the bottle. You hear a whoosh as bubbles escape. When poured, it takes the shape of a glass. Bubbles float up and escape. What is a fizzy drink?

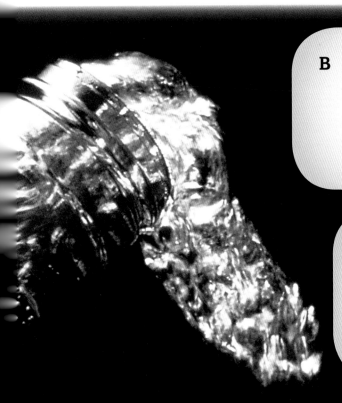

B A teacher writes with chalk. Then, she wipes off the writing. What is chalk?

C Make a ball with a special putty. Put the putty over a hole. It slowly drips through. What is putty?

Answers:

A A fizzy drink is a mixture of liquid and gas. When a bottle is opened, gas escapes into the air.

B Chalk is a solid. When rubbed against a board, tiny chalk pieces stick to the board. Each piece is a solid.

C Putty is a special liquid. Like a solid, it keeps its shape for a short time. But given enough time, it flows like a liquid.

Glossary

atom smallest unit of matter. Atoms are too small to see.

boil reach a temperature at which a liquid changes to a gas

compress press tightly together. Gases are compressed when they are put in a smaller container.

condense cause a gas to change to a liquid. Water vapour sometimes condenses on a cold glass.

energy ability to make something happen. Energy can make things move or change shape.

evaporate change from liquid into a gas. Puddles evaporate in the sun.

freeze change from liquid to solid by loss of heat. Water freezes at 0 °C (32 °F).

gas matter that spreads apart and fills any container. The air we breathe is made of gases.

lava liquid rock flowing out of a volcano. Lava is very hot.

liquid matter that flows and can change shape. A liquid always takes up the same amount of space.

magma liquid rock underground. When it comes to the surface, it is called lava.

matter anything that takes up space and can be weighed. Everything on Earth is made of matter.

melt reach a temperature at which a solid changes to a liquid

mixture blend of two or more materials. A mixture can be separated again.

particle tiny part of something. Atoms are the smallest particles of matter.

solid substance with a definite shape. A solid always takes up the same amount of space.

state form of matter. Solid, liquid, and gas are the three states of matter.

tar material used for paving. Tar is a very thick liquid.

vapour gas. Water vapour can make the air feel humid.

volume amount of space something takes up

Want to know more?

Books to read

• *Building Blocks of Matter: Atoms and Molecules*, Louise and Richard Spilsbury (Heinemann Library, 2007)

• *Science Answers: Solids, Liquids and Gases*, Chris Oxlade (Heinemann Library, 2003).

Websites

• www.chem.purdue.edu/gchelp/atoms/states.html
This website gives you a microscopic view of different states of matter.

• www.bbc.co.uk/schools/ks2bitesize/science/materials.shtml
Do an activity and watch particles move in matter.

Learn all about atoms and molecules in *Fighter Jet.*

Find out how states of matter can help you survive on a desert island in a *A Matter of Survival.*

Index